AF428247

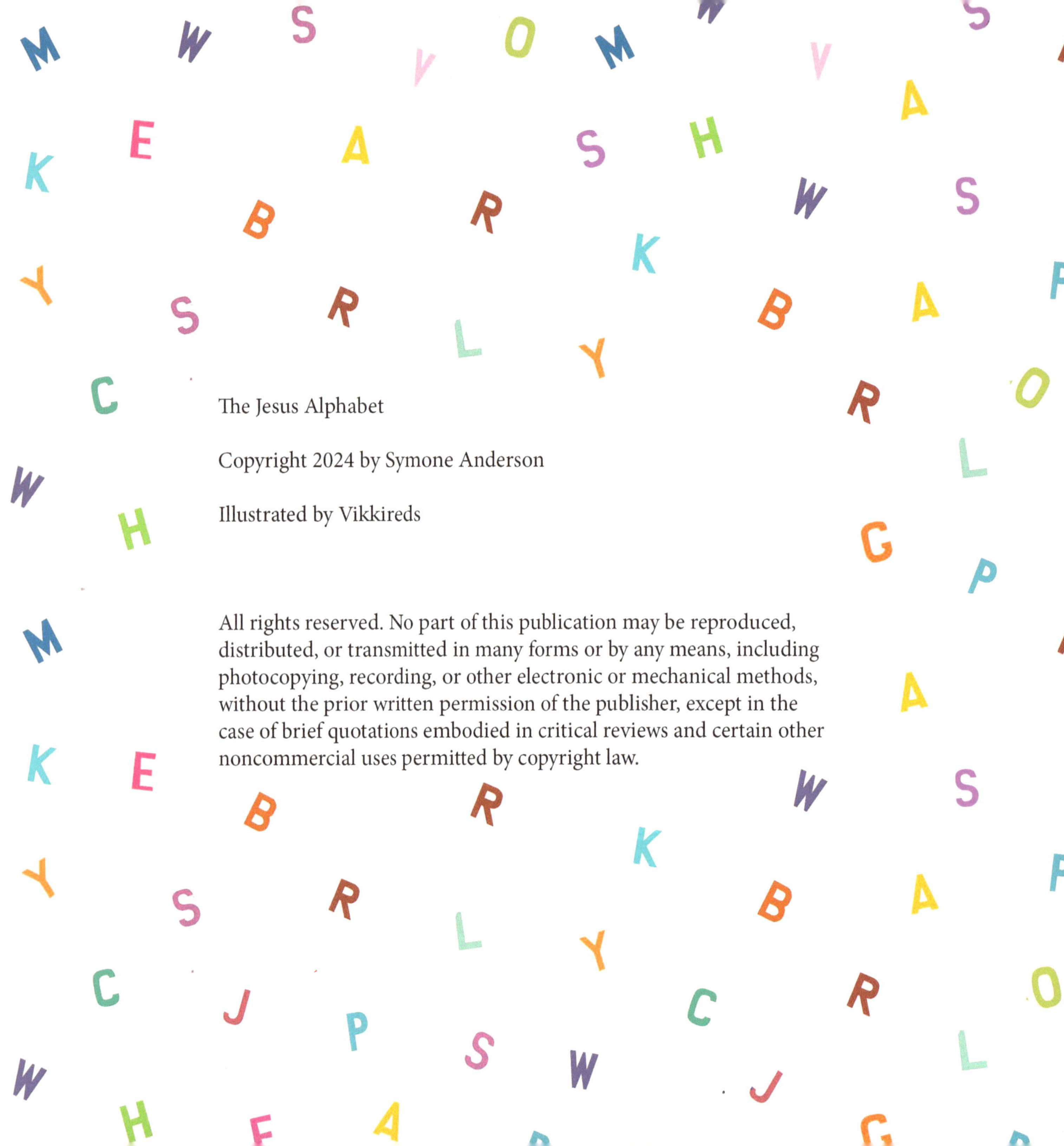

The Jesus Alphabet

Copyright 2024 by Symone Anderson

Illustrated by Vikkireds

WRITTEN BY SYMONE ANDERSON

The Jesus

ALPHABET

FROM A TO Z

ILLUSTRATED BY VIKKIREDS

Jesus is **ALPHA**,
the beginning of each morning,
the start of my day.

Jesus is BEAUTIFUL; an amazing sight to see.

Jesus is COMPASSIONATE
to all who come around.
LOVE

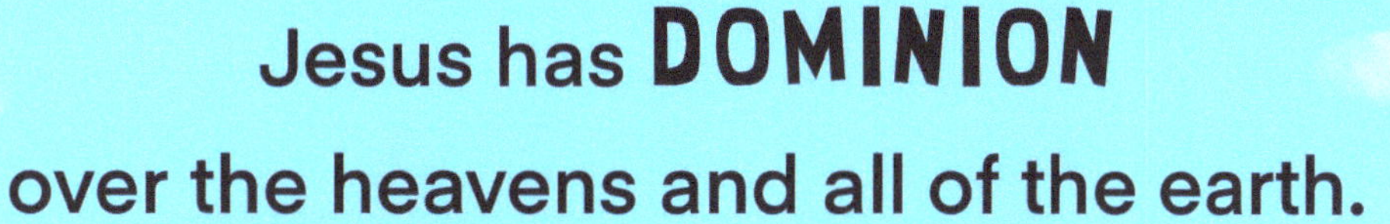

Jesus has DOMINION
over the heavens and all of the earth.

Jesus is **ETERNAL**,
He will live through and through every
month, every season, and every year too.

Jesus is **FAITHFUL** to His words and promises He keeps.

Jesus is GRACIOUS, full of
mercy renewed just for me.

Jesus is HOLY, set apart, above all creation.

Jesus is **INSPIRING** to everyone to be humble and to always serve one another.

Jesus is **JOYOUS,** full of unconditional love,
especially for me.

Jesus is **KIND** to everyone,
spreading the Gospel to those
who will hear.

Jesus is a great **LISTENER** to your prayers no matter the time of night or day.

Jesus is MIRACULOUS, wonderous presence, a shining light of hope to many.

Jesus is always **NEAR**, close to those who call to Him for help.

Jesus is **OMEGA**, He is there
for the ending to every second,
every minute and hour.

Jesus is ALL-POWERFUL LORD
and Savior of all people.

Jesus is QUALIFIED because
He died for our sins on Calvary.

Jesus is **RIGHTEOUS**, full of justice; to correct
each wrong and set things right.

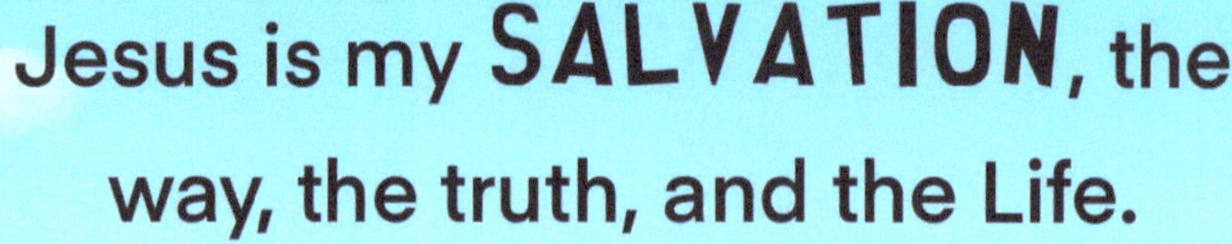
Jesus is my SALVATION, the
way, the truth, and the Life.

Jesus is a TEACHER,
revealing truth about the world
that surrounds me.

Jesus is **UNDERSTANDING** of the feelings I
have whether big or small.

Jesus is VICTORIOUS
because He has overcome the enemy.

Jesus is **WORTHY** of all worship and praise every day no matter where I am.

HALLELUJAH!
We worship and praise you Jesus!
LOVE

Jesus is EXALTED high above the earth.

Jesus is always with **YOU** and me from the beginning right to the very end.

He is everything that I will ever need all the way
from A down to the letter Z .

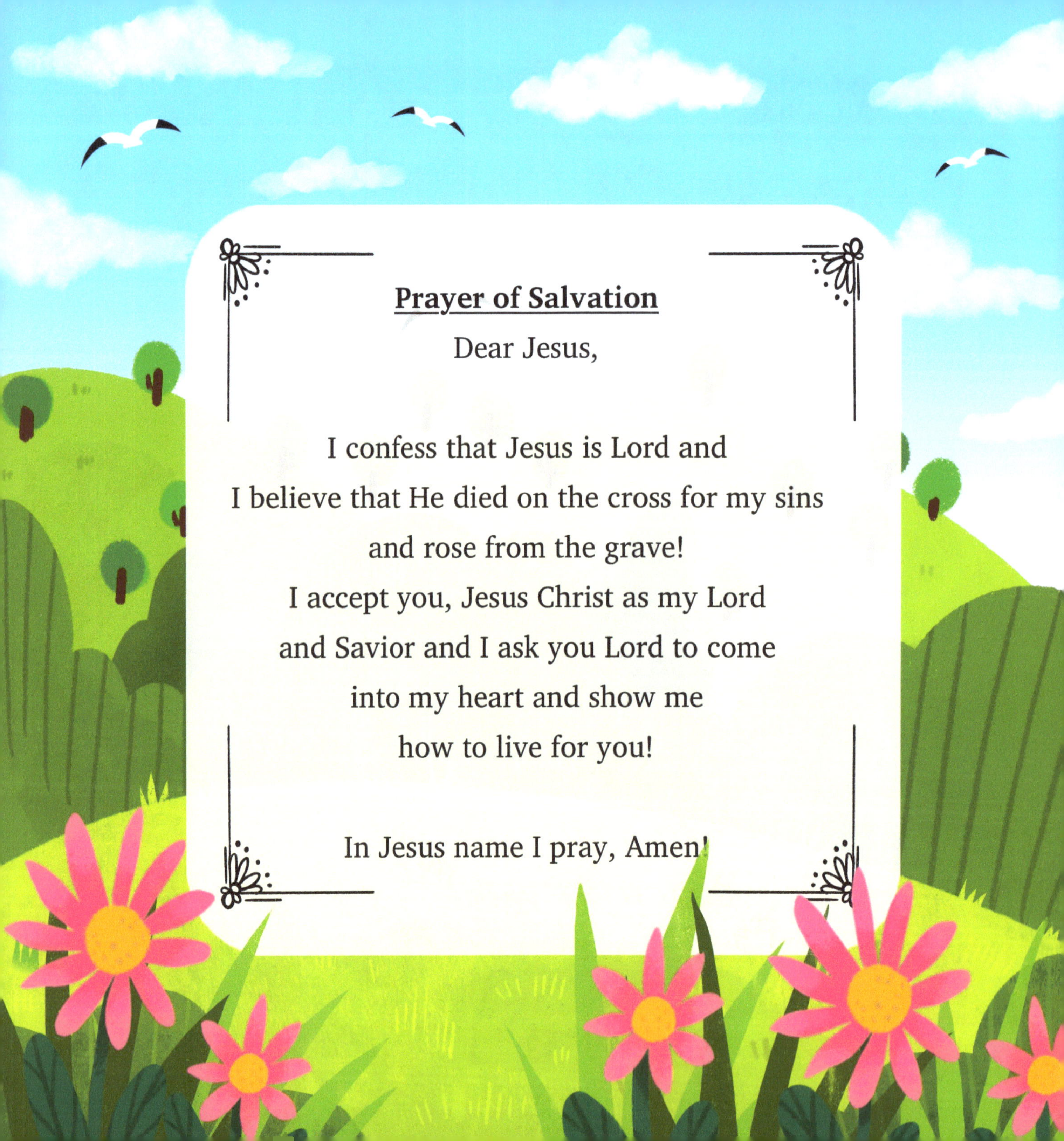
Prayer of Salvation
Dear Jesus,

I confess that Jesus is Lord and
I believe that He died on the cross for my sins
and rose from the grave!
I accept you, Jesus Christ as my Lord
and Savior and I ask you Lord to come
into my heart and show me
how to live for you!

In Jesus name I pray, Amen!